A Shadow Line Of My Own

Alex Gonzalez

Made with ❤ on the BookLeaf Publishing Platform
www.bookleafpub.in
www.bookleafpub.com

Dedication

This is for You ...

Preface

This is my maiden voyage into sharing and putting my writing out there in the ether. I can only hope that it touches.
In all gratitude,
Thank you,
Alex

Acknowledgements

To All that love me,
have loved me, suffered me
supported me throughout my life,
I'd like to say again;
This is for You.

1. Flame

I am on fire
Been set ablaze
Won't you come
Around and stay
A bit
And
Warm yourself
Around my flames

2. Jukebox Heart

I just play
On repeat

Love songs
In this
Jukebox of a heart

Sometimes
the songs
run out

I always have
though

Another
Pretty
Shiny coin

To place
back
In the slot

3. Until when?

A ride home with friends
Empty conversations and
Fleeting glances

Until when?
A parking lot
And the lost sound of a train

Refuge found us
This covering tree

We've got wet asphalt
and maybe a dream

Got drawn into
parking lot spaces

And we're both here
Somewhere in between
Yellow painted lines
And your
Soul filled eyes
Until when?

All these thoughts that clamor
around our heads
just like
the rain

Until when?
And then

you just lean in ...

4. Storms on the Sun

5

Tucked into dreams
Long and true
These songs came to bare

Music
Melody
Views
Of you
That dance with the light

Images
Unfold
Frame by frame
Scene by scene

Just like you remembered
about the young
the seasons

All of those
Storms on the Sun

5. A Twilight Scene

Stay right there
just like that
just right there

Movement
means a stirring
that defies
picture perfect

Stay right there
just like that
A pose
meant for a dream

Changing
is a chance
to take, that
we just don't need

Nowhere
needs an appointment from us
to go
anywhere

Until a morning

A morning far away
at the earliest
At the least ...

6. Gasoline Dream

Tongue's tied
With wishes
tone deaf and
tripping over
 souls
of dreams

Made it
to the car
now to keep
the engine running
in the cold and still

Made it up
this far
with a burning
motor
in the dark
up on blocks
ramps
and down

Pulled this thing
onto the

interstate
just to keep running
with a song
and a thought

Gasoline
spilling
all the way
long road
to mark my path
back home

Package full of matches
sitting shotgun
waiting for
that just so
to let that spark

Go.

7. Ransom Note

Put it all down
piece by piece
like a ransom note
cut, glued and pasted

It's what you want
building blocks
assembled

A temple
within
reaching new heights

Pass code: Allowed

8. Lightning Bug

Captured
a fairy
in a jar

Knowing
it's where she's not supposed to be
Resisting
the urge
from
twisting the lid off

Free or
Under lock and key?
Willingly

What would you suffer
and risk

To keep her close
just to taste
and feel

Honey trickled
on

A razors edge

Days on end

9. At Closing Time

Counting my steps
in the night
because I'll need them

The information
the data

For that walk
down the hall

For that dance on the floor
and a kiss
for the stealing

Learning to move
in the dark
When all you have
is a heartbeat
for sight

It will come again though

Adjust for light

10. Dusk, Dawn and Done

Morning brings
awakening and
a scattering
of dreams

Bright warnings of
unbridled roads
and whispers of care

Taken the path
to where
the road spills out
right in front of you

Like a thrilling book
yet to be written
or read

Turn the pages
as it leaves
it's lessons
in lines and time

Dirt

on the roads
behind

                                              15

Forever is now
and
Forever means more

11. Given

Born
of stone, earth and star

You remember you
a fold in time
a simple crease
in a scar

At your own tempo
finding flight

An offering up
of a heart on fire
with both hands
to all above

And to rain
down
below

12. Finish the Dance

Finish the dance
all to the beat
of her heart

Finish the dance
all to the beat
of her love

Stare into those eyes
that gaze of strength
beauty defying definition
that pierces and fills

Lose sleep
at the thought of dreaming
and make it
so

All to the beat
of her heart
and soul

Finish the dance

13. Today

And then
tomorrow begins

When you weren't even done
with today

Let alone
Yesterday

14. I Am the Storm

Falling - Falling
spiral
twisting body boy
in the air

Drifting
down now
through this
atmosphere

Watching
for signs
of the divine
and canceled flights

My vision
clearly blurred

Looking
to make
Landfall soon

15. Dead Sexy

She just shakes her head
when she hears them say,
"Well, she's just dead sexy" they say

She takes her walks at night
all the streetlights
are her friends
them, and the shadows

He says;
"Thank you, I'll never forget this"
as he crosses the road
ignoring the red

To the train tracks
to wrest

Waiting in the darkness
for the next ride
to hit

16. Dial In

I'll take the daylight
with its promised
subsequence

As I try to
Capture
that prize
of a little of
today

In fragments
one storm
one rainbow
one day
a night
at a time

I can use it as a frequency
A number on the dial

Tuned in for the next episode

Same channel
Same time ...

17. My Air

Until
There is no more

Air to take in
or a breath
to breathe out

No more
second thoughts
left
Without you there

Without you there

Well,

All is at
stake

18. Any Day

When tomorrow promised
and today came
to take it all away

Yesterday
still wants to talk

About all
that's gone astray

19. No Romeo

There is no Romeo here
on that midnight call

There's no "I love you"
Just a sliced window screen
and a crawling inside

There is
No Romeo here

Just a little demon
with a little problem
that's named "you"

Already ready
to cast you aside
before you knew

20. Fast Insects

A scattering of thought
memory and dreams

Just like
fast insects

Maybe
worthy of capture

gathering them
sheperd them
Quick insects, reptiles
wind and rain

All
At hands reach

Find a bait

Catch them and
keep them here
to explain
of all the secrets

Above
and
Below

21. Catching Flies

Turns out
I made a new friend today

He's a gecko
named Sigmund
at least
that's what he said

I just so happened
to be catching flies
that day
while he rested
in my coffee cup
being fed

I know that
I have to let him
go

But
there's no reason why
I don't think

There's any reason

to send a new friend away
back home
on an
empty stomach

www.ingramcontent.com/pod-product-compliance
Lightning Source LLC
LaVergne TN
LVHW010022200726
843495LV00015B/1884